A GUIDE TO READING
SHAKESPEARE'S *THE TEMPEST*

A GUIDE TO READING
SHAKESPEARE'S *THE TEMPEST*

MARIA FRANZISKA FAHEY

Maria Franziska Fahey is the author of *Metaphor and Shakespearean Drama: Unchaste Signification*, which was shortlisted for the 2012 Shakespeare's Globe Book Award. She is a member of the faculty at Friends Seminary, where she has taught English for more than twenty years.

First Printing, 2013
Second Printing, 2013, contains a new preface, reorganized appendices, and minor revisions of the text.

ISBN-13: 978-0615833569
ISBN-10: 061583356X

Accabonac Press
61 Jane Street, Suite 17C, New York, NY 10014

Cover illustration and design by Lauren Simkin Berke

CONTENTS

PREFACE

On the Pleasures & Challenges of Reading Shakespeare's Dramatic Language

Reading Shakespeare's plays can be immensely pleasurable, but doing so is no easy task. Whereas we now get a great deal of our information through visual images, including photographs and film, in Shakespeare's day most information came through spoken language. Part of the fun, and also the challenge, of reading a Shakespeare play is having to transform language into visual images for ourselves.

Indeed, Shakespeare was aware of the demands he was making of his audiences. In the Prologue to his play *The Life of Henry the Fifth*, the Chorus admits that it cannot bring King Henry himself or "the vasty fields of France" into the theater and so asks the members of the audience to let the play work on their "imaginary forces" (*Henry V* Pro. 12, 18). The Chorus goes on to suggest, "Think, when we talk of horses, that you see them, / Printing their proud hoofs i'th' receiving earth" (Pro. 26-7).

A Shakespeare play is largely "talk"—a series of conversations among a cast of characters. However, the talk of a Shakespeare play is often more difficult to understand than ordinary speech because it has been crafted to bring a whole world before our eyes. The series of questions in this guide is designed to help you listen carefully, scene-by-scene, to what the characters say so that you can use your "imaginary forces" to see the world of *The Tempest* for yourself. As you read the play's language and begin to envision its world, it will be helpful to remain aware of how the language spoken by characters in the play is different from that of ordinary speech. Here are a few of these differences:

Vocabulary. Written over 400 years ago, the plays are known for their unusually large vocabularies, including many words that were, at the time, new to the English language—some probably invented by Shakespeare himself. Almost all readers find the rich vocabulary of a Shakespeare play challenging to understand even as they come to enjoy the subtle and abundant connotations of the words Shakespeare chose. Furthermore, twenty-first century readers will find that the meanings of some words have changed since Shakespeare's day and that other words, rarely spoken now, have become obsolete. For instance, the word *luggage* in Caliban's question, "what do you mean / To dote thus on such luggage" (4.1.230), refers to anything that has to be lugged about—not necessarily to the baggage of a traveller. Be sure to consult the notes in your copy of the play and to keep a good dictionary at hand, one that provides older meanings of words. (Check your library's print or online version of *The Oxford English Dictionary*—the *OED*—which is the most comprehensive English dictionary.)

But don't feel obligated to look up every word when first reading a play. You can understand a great deal about unfamiliar words from their context. Consider, for instance, the context of the word *sot* in Caliban's remark about Prospero:

> Remember
> First to possess his books, for without them
> He's but a sot [.]   (*Tempest* 3.2.87-9)

You might not know what a *sot* is. But you can figure out that if Caliban imagines that Prospero will be only a *sot* without his books, then a *sot* must be a person who does not read books and does not, therefore, know as much as she or he might. (The *Oxford English Dictionary* defines *sot* as "A foolish or stupid person" (*OED* 1).)

⌒⚓ Poetic Language. The conversations in a Shakespeare play are no ordinary conversations: they were crafted by a poet-playwright who used sound, rhythm, and imagery to convey his meanings. Consider the lines spoken by Prospero at the end of the play's epilogue:

> As you from crimes would pardoned be,
> Let your indulgence set me free.　　　(*Tempest* Epi. 19-20)

In ordinary speech, someone would likely say, "As you *would be pardoned* from crimes." But Shakespeare's word order allows the lines to rhyme—"be" with "free"—which adds a finality to Prospero's request and to the epilogue. Furthermore, Prospero's speeches within the play are not composed in couplets whereas the epilogue is. This difference distinguishes the Prospero who speaks the epilogue to an audience of *The Tempest* from the Prospero who speaks to other characters within the play-world. (*See page 75 of appendix 1 for an explanation of* couplet.)

⌒⚓ Descriptions that Provide Context. Although Shakespeare's theater included costumes and some props, it did not include sets or lighting. (The use of electricity was centuries away, and plays were performed at The Globe, an open-air theater, in the mid-afternoon.) Audiences would have to glean important context from the characters' speeches. For instance, in act 1, scene 2 of *The Tempest*, we hear a description of the storm at sea when Miranda asks her father to calm ("allay") it. Her request includes the poetic description of a sky so dark that it seems to pour down hot tar ("pitch") and a sea so stormy that waves seem to reach up to the sky ("welkin") as if to put the "fire" (perhaps of lightning) out:

> If by your art, my dearest father, you have
> Put the wild waters in this roar, allay them.
> The sky it seems would pour down stinking pitch,
> But that the sea, mounting to th'welkin's cheek,
> Dashes the fire out.　　　(*Tempest* 1.2.1-5)

Nowadays such images of a storm at sea could be shown to a theater audience through lighting design, sets, and special effects. Thus, contemporary playwrights usually don't write such descriptions into characters' speeches, and contemporary audiences don't have to decipher and picture them.

⌒⚓ Implied Action. Unlike stories or novels, most plays don't have a narrator who tells us what characters are doing as they speak to each other. Playwrights can indicate specific actions with stage directions, but Shakespeare's plays have relatively few. Instead, the dialogue itself gives clues about characters' actions. Consider the exchange between Miranda and Prospero when Miranda is trying to persuade her father to be nicer to Ferdinand. (*Beseech* here means "I beg"; *hence* means "go away.")

> *Miranda*　　　　　　　　Beseech you, father!
> *Prospero*　　　Hence! Hang not on my garments.　　　(*Tempest* 1.2.475-6)

Prospero's line lets us see that as Miranda begs, she physically is holding onto her father's clothing. Imagining the world of a Shakespeare play depends, in part, on listening for clues to characters' actions. (Try staging a scene with some friends: doing so will help you become attentive to such clues.)

Learning to see the world of a Shakespeare play by reading or hearing its language takes some work and some patience. However, paying close attention to the play's language will give you access to the most interesting, complicated, and surprising aspects of the plays. As the Prologue to *The Life of Henry the Fifth* shows, Shakespeare invited and relied on his audiences to envision the worlds of his plays, and Shakespeare gave us incomparable language from which to do so. There are always many ways to imagine a phrase, line, or scene, but it's important to start with accurate observations of the play's language.

Using This Guide

The series of questions for each scene will help you to observe the sometimes complex and dense language accurately and to puzzle through the characters' conversations. Before trying to answer the questions for a particular scene, read through the entire scene aloud. Or, better yet, gather some friends, take parts, and read the scene aloud together. Don't be shy: you might mispronounce a word or need to read some lines slowly, but you will have a much better chance of understanding the lines when you read them aloud—and you likely will have more fun. Then, read through the scene again slowly, answering the questions as you go. If you don't fully understand a question, quote the phrase or line that you suspect contains the clues for its answer. Once you reach the scene's end, return to those questions to see if you have been able to figure out anything further.

Some of the questions use terms and refer to methods with which you may not be familiar: they may ask you to observe and analyze "meter" or "figurative language," especially "metaphor." Don't worry if you are not familiar with these terms or if you never have "scanned a line of verse" or "sorted a metaphor's tenor and vehicle": you will find the necessary background information and sample analyses in the appendices. Appendix 1, "Listening for Meter," explains how to identify the basic rhythms of Shakespeare's poetry; appendix 2, "Reading Figurative Language," explains how to identify and analyze figures of speech; and appendix 3, "On How an Edition of *The Tempest* Is Made," explains how the copy of *The Tempest* you are reading is derived from the earliest texts of the play and lets you know what kinds of additions and changes an editor may have made in preparing the play for publication. You may find it helpful to read through these appendices before you begin to answer the questions. Or you may consult them when you arrive at a question that requires your knowledge of the information they provide. All of the information in the appendices aims to help you to understand and envision the play for yourself.

Quotations in this guide are taken from the edition of *The Tempest* edited by Burton Raffel and published by Yale University Press in 2006. Following standard scholarly practice, quotations are followed by a citation that indicates the act, scene, and lines from which a passage is quoted. So, for instance, "(3.1.6-7)" refers to act 3, scene 1, lines 6-7. If you are reading a different edition of the play, your line numbers may be slightly different. *(See appendix 3, "On How an Edition of* The Tempest *Is Made," for an explanation of how the differences in editions come about.)*

Hearing & Seeing Performances

If, after trying to read aloud by yourself and with friends, you continue to have trouble getting the gist of what the characters are saying to each other, try to locate a good audio recording of the play, one that has been recorded by a cast of experienced Shakespearean actors. (Many libraries have them available.) Read along as you listen to the audio recording of the scene you are working on. Hearing trained actors deliver the characters' lines will likely help you understand much of what the characters are saying. Keep in mind that the way an actor speaks a line depends on that actor's interpretation of it and that you might have another interpretation.

After reading the play, you might enjoy seeing a performance of it. Check to see if there is a live performance at a nearby theater, or borrow a film of the play from your library. If you wait to see a performance until after reading the play, you will be able to compare the way you have imagined the play-world to the way a particular director has. If you see the performance before you've read the play, be aware, as you read, that the particular director's vision of the play is not the only possibility: one good way to do so is to see two, or more, performances or films.

There are many books and websites that publish summaries and analyses of Shakespeare's plays. Be wary. Don't accept another reader's vision of the play too easily: your own careful reading and imagining might lead you to a far more interesting one!

QUESTIONS TO CONSIDER AS YOU READ *THE TEMPEST*

Larger Questions

As you answer the questions for each scene, you often will be prompted to think about the topics listed below. If you are particularly interested in one of these topics, you might find it helpful to keep track of what various characters say about it by marking relevant passages in your text or by keeping a list of relevant passages in a notebook. When you have finished reading the play, you then will be ready to consider the collection of passages you have gathered and ask yourself what the play as a whole might be suggesting about the topic. This kind of work is one way to prepare to write an essay about *The Tempest*.

1. **Strangers.** How do various characters respond to encounters with strangers? How do they perceive strangers? What prompts characters to reconsider their first impressions of a stranger?

2. **Power.** How do characters gain power over others? How do they maintain it? What deals do characters make in efforts to gain power?

3. **Social Relations & Hierarchies**. How are social hierarchies established? When do they change? Under what conditions might a hierarchy be overturned, even temporarily? How are previous hierarchies reestablished?

4. **Status & Property.** How do various characters obtain status and property? (Inheritance from parents? Birth place? Knowledge? Special skills? Might? Violence? Gender? Age?) How do characters justify status and property they claim as rightly theirs? How are contracts used?

5. **Servitude & Bondage, Freedom & Liberty.** What makes some characters subservient to or enslaved by others? What keeps them so? Which characters reject subservience? When? Which characters embrace subservience? When? What deals do characters make in efforts to gain liberty?

6. **Transformation.** Who changes and how? What forces transform characters?

7. **Revenge & Forgiveness.** What prompts revenge? What motivates forgiveness? What do characters say about vengeance and fury? About reason? About grace?

8. **Magic & Sorcery.** What is Prospero's magic? How does it work? Who else uses or is said to use magic or sorcery? What kinds? What other than magic is said to be enchanting?

9. **Spectacles, Pageants, & Theater.** What is the role of spectacle and pageant within the world of the play? What about music?

10. **Visions & Dreams.** What do characters say about visions and dreams?

11. **Fate, Fortune, Providence, & Destiny.** What do characters say about destiny? About the gods?

12. **Knowledge, Language, & Books.** What do characters say about knowledge and ignorance? About self-knowledge? What do characters say about language? About Prospero's books?

Patterns of Figurative Language

Questions for each scene also will prompt you to notice and analyze figurative language. *(See appendix 1 for an introduction to figurative language.)* Sometimes one instance of figurative language echoes figurative language from other scenes in the play. These patterns of figurative language are an important part of how the play is structured and delivers its meanings. You might find it helpful to keep track of repeating figures by marking instances of them in your text or by keeping a list in a notebook. When you have finished reading the play, you then will be ready to ask yourself what the pattern suggests or means. In *The Tempest*, be on the lookout for figures of:

1. **Cycles in Nature:** ebbing and flowing, night and day

2. **Theater:** cast, perform, act, prologue

3. **Disease:** canker, infect, plague

ACT 1, SCENE 1

1. As the play opens, what is happening on the ship (1.1.1-8)? Who is in charge?

2. What does the Boatswain ask King Alonso to do and then order Antonio to do?

3. To whom does Gonzalo refer when he cautions the Boatswain, "remember whom thou hast aboard" (1.1.19)?

4. Gonzalo tells the Boatswain: "If you can command these elements to silence, and work the peace of the present, we will not hand a rope more, use your authority" (1.1.21-3). What does the Boatswain suggest here that Gonzalo should do if he is so able? With what tone might the Boatswain say this?

5. What alternative does the Boatswain suggest when he continues, "If you cannot, give thanks you have lived so long, and make yourself ready in your cabin for the mischance of the hour, if it so hap" (1.1.23-6)?

6. Reread 1.1.27-32 ("I have great comfort . . . our case is miserable"). Why does Gonzalo hope it is the Boatswain's fate to be hanged? (There was a proverb, in Shakespeare's day, that those born to be hanged would not be drowned.)

7. What is the Boatswain's attitude toward Sebastian and Antonio? What is Sebastian and Antonio's attitude toward the Boatswain? Quote the lines from which you derive your answer.

8. Gonzalo expresses certainty that the Boatswain will not drown: "I'll warrant him for drowning, though the ship were no stronger than a nutshell, and as leaky as an unstanched wench" (1.1.44-6). To what does Gonzalo compare a potentially leaky ship? What does this comparison imply about what makes a wench dangerous? (A "wench" is a *girl* or *young woman* (*OED* 1).)

9. When the ship begins to "split," Antonio says, "Let's all sink wi'the King" (1.1.63). How does Sebastian respond? What does this response suggest about Sebastian?

10. Review the scene and consider the ship's hierarchy. Assign a number to the following characters with "1" for the most power and "4" for the least.

_____ Master

_____ Boatswain

_____ Alonso

_____ Gonzalo

Jot down the most important lines from which you derive your answers along with some notes about your reasoning. Include notes on what, if anything, makes it difficult to rank any of the characters.

11. How might the ship's hierarchy be different in calm weather? How might the hierarchy be different if these same men were on land?

ACT 1, SCENE 2

1. What does Miranda ask her father to do "If by [his] art" he has "Put the wild waters in this roar" (1.2.1-2)?

2. With what kind of "art" might Prospero have done so?

3. How does Miranda react to the shipwreck? What does she say she would have done if she "had been any god of power" (1.2.10)?

4. How does Prospero reassure Miranda that "there is no soul—/ No, not so much perdition as an hair—/Betid to any creature in the vessel" (1.2.29-31)? What does Prospero say he has done to be sure?

5. How old was Miranda when they came "unto this cell" (1.2.39)?

6. What does Miranda remember of that time? What does she not remember?

7. For how long have Prospero and Miranda been on the island?

8. How old is Miranda now?

9. What prompts Miranda to ask, "Sir, are not you my father" (1.2.55)? What does her question suggest about Prospero as he is now?

10. Explain Prospero's answer, "Thy mother was a piece of virtue, and / She said thou wast my daughter" (1.2.56-7). What does Miranda's mother's virtue have to do with Prospero's being her father?

11. What had been Prospero's position in Milan?

12. Why had Prospero "cast" the government on his brother, Antonio (1.2.75)? Cite the lines in which you find your answers.

13. Prospero explains what happened as Antonio performed the duties of duke: "now he was / The ivy which had hid my princely trunk / And sucked my verdure out on't" (1.2.85-7). Make a sketch of this metaphor that shows both its vehicle and tenor. *(See pages 79-85 of appendix 1, "Reading Figurative Language," for explanations of these terms and methods.)*

14. Then, chart the metaphor's vehicle and tenor.

<u>vehicle</u>	:	<u>tenor</u>
ivy	:	he (Antonio)
	:	
	:	
	:	

15. Reread Prospero's explanation of what happened to his brother:

> like one
> Who having into truth, by telling of it,
> Made such a sinner of his memory
> To credit his own lie, he did believe
> He was indeed the Duke, out o' the substitution
> And executing th'outward face of royalty
> With all prerogative. (1.2.99-105)

a. How, according to Prospero, did his brother come to believe "He was indeed the Duke"?

b. How, according to Prospero, can one's memory be a sinner?

c. In what way did Antonio's memory sin? How did it "credit his own lie"?

d. What is Prospero's theory of what can happen when someone acts a role—when he "execute[s] th' outward face" of that role?

16. What does Prospero say was "dukedom large enough" for him (1.2.110)?

17. What does Prospero lament happened to "poor Milan" as a result of Antonio's plot (1.2.115)?

18. As he starts to tell Miranda the details of Antonio's plot, Prospero asks Miranda to tell him if someone who acted this way "might be a brother" (1.2.117-18). Miranda responds, "I should sin / To think but nobly of my grandmother. / Good wombs have borne bad sons" (1.2.118-20). How does Miranda understand Prospero's question? (Do you think she understands it as Prospero intends it?) What does Miranda say about mothers and sons?

19. Reread 1.2.120-7 ("Now the conditions . . . With all the honors, on my brother."). Be sure to read your notes. Then explain:

   a. What "suit" of Prospero's brother, Antonio, did the King of Naples "hearke[n]"?

   b. What does Antonio gain from the deal?

   c. At what cost?

   d. What does the King of Naples gain?

20. What did a "treacherous army" do to complete the plan (1.2.128)?

21. What does Prospero explain when Miranda wonders why "they" did not "destroy" her and her father (1.2.138)?

22. How does Prospero respond to Miranda's worry that she must have been trouble to her father?

23. What is Prospero's response to Miranda's question, "How came we ashore" (1.2.158)? Quote the line.

24. How did Prospero come to have clothes and books with him on the island?

25. According to Prospero, how, on the island, did Miranda "profit" more "than other princes can" (1.2.172-3)?

26. When Miranda asks his "reason / For raising this sea-storm" (1.2.176-7), Prospero tells her that Fortune has brought his "enemies . . to this shore" (1.2.179-80), but he then puts her to sleep (1.2.186). What might motivate Prospero to do so at this moment?

27. What do we learn about Ariel's relationship to Prospero from the way Ariel greets him (1.2.189-93)?

28. Review Ariel's description of the shipwreck (1.2.196-206). How would you describe the language he uses? Begin your answer by quoting one or two specific phrases.

29. Given what Prospero tells Miranda earlier (1.2.30), how would you account for Prospero's asking Ariel if the people who were on the ship are safe (1.2.217)?

30. Where are the passengers from the shipwreck? Where is the King's son?

31. Ariel tells Prospero that he has hidden the King's ship "in the deep nook, where once / Thou call'dst me up at midnight to fetch dew / From the still-vexed Bermoothes" (1.2.227-9). Scholars have understood "Bermoothes" as a variant spelling of *Bermuda*. What did Prospero once ask Ariel to do in Bermoothes?

32. Where is the rest of the fleet? What do the passengers aboard those ships think happened to the king's ship?

33. When Ariel tells Prospero that the time is "Past the mid season" (1.2.239), Prospero adds, "At least two glasses" (1.2.239-40). Prospero then tells Ariel that they have more work "'twixt six and now" (1.2.240). (Here "mid season" means *noon*; "glasses" refer to *hour-glasses*.) What time is it? Until when does Prospero say they will work?

34. On what basis does Ariel demand his liberty?

35. How does Prospero respond to Ariel's demand? Does Prospero deny Ariel's claim?

36. Reread 1.2.257-94 ("Thou liest, malignant thing! . . . When I arrived, and heard thee, that made gape / The pine, and let thee out.").

    a. How does Prospero describe Sycorax? Quote and cite a phrase or two.

    b. Note that "Argier" was a variant spelling of *Algiers*. Why, according to Prospero, did Sycorax leave Argier? Why was she banished instead of killed?

    c. Why, according to Prospero, did Sycorax "confine" Ariel "Into a cloven pine" (1.2.275-8)?

    d. Who is Sycorax's son?

e. Slowly reread Prospero's sentence with the tricky syntax. ("Save" here means *except*.)

> Then was this island
> (Save for the son, that she did litter here,
> A freckled whelp, hag-born) not honored with
> A human shape. (1.2.282-4)

1. At the time Ariel was left imprisoned in the pine, the island was not "honored" with a "human shape" except whose?

2. What does Prospero thus imply about Caliban's shape?

3. Is Prospero's use of "litter" and "whelp" literal or figurative? Explain your reasoning.

37. Compare the story Prospero tells about Sycorax and Caliban and their arrival onto the island to the story he tells about his and Miranda's arrival. Compare the parent-child pairs. Parallels? Differences? Chart your points of comparison.

Sycorax and Caliban	Prospero and Miranda
_____	_____
_____	_____
_____	_____
_____	_____
_____	_____
_____	_____
_____	_____
_____	_____
_____	_____
_____	_____

38. How was Ariel released from the pine?

39. With what does Prospero threaten Ariel? What does he promise? What new order does he give Ariel?

40. What happens immediately before Prospero awakens Miranda?

41. How does Prospero respond to Miranda's comment that Caliban is "a villain" that she does "not love to look on" (1.2.310-11)?

42. How does Prospero address Caliban? How does Caliban respond?

43. What prompts Prospero to say he'll punish Caliban with "cramps" (1.2.326)?

44. On what basis does Caliban claim, "This island's mine" (1.2.332-3)? Quote the relevant phrase.

45. How, according to Caliban, did Prospero treat him when he first came to the island (1.2.333-7)?

46. What does Caliban say he did for Prospero then (1.2.337-9)?

47. How does Caliban feel about having done so now (1.2.340)?

48. Until what event, according to Prospero, had he lodged Caliban in his own cell (1.2.345-9)?

49. "Oh ho, oh ho, would't had been done!" (1.2.350).

    a. How does Caliban respond to Prospero's accusation? What does Caliban say he wishes "had been done"?

    b. What is Caliban's reason for wishing so? Quote the line.

50. Reread 1.2.352-9 ("Abhorrèd slave . . . With words that made them known.")

    a. What does Miranda say she did for Caliban when she "pitied" him when he would "gabble like / A thing most brutish" (1.2.354-8)?

    b. What might have been Caliban's "gabbl[ing]"? List two possibilities.

    c. What specifically might Miranda have taught Caliban? List two possibilities.

51. Why, according to Caliban, must he obey Prospero (1.2.373-5)?

52. Reread Ariel's songs (1.2.375-88, 1.2.398-404). About what does he sing?

53. How does Ferdinand react to the songs?

54. How does Miranda react to Ferdinand when she first sees him (1.2.411-13)?

55. How does Ferdinand react to Miranda (1.2.423-4)?

56. Who is Ferdinand's father? What does Ferdinand think has happened to him?

57. Prospero comments of Miranda and Ferdinand that "At the first sight / They have changed eyes" (1.2.442-3).

    a.   What does he mean by "changed eyes"?

    b.   How does he feel about their "chang[ing] eyes"? Cite your evidence.

58. Wondering why her father speaks to Ferdinand "so ungently" Miranda says, "This / Is the third man that e'er I saw, the first / That e'er I sighed for" (1.2.446-8).

    a.   Who, then, would be the first and second men Miranda has seen?

    b.   As what, thus, does Miranda identify Caliban?

59. What does Ferdinand offer Miranda (1.2.449-51)? With what condition?

60. Of what does Prospero accuse Ferdinand ("Thou dost here usurp . . . the lord on't" (1.2.455-8))?

61. What motivates Prospero to accuse Ferdinand? (Reread 1.2.452-4 ("They are both in either's powers . . . Make the prize light") to discover the answer.)

62. How does Ferdinand try to "resist such entertainment" as Prospero threatens (1.2.467)? What happens when he tries to resist?

63. How does Miranda react to her father's actions toward Ferdinand?

64. What does Prospero mean when he says to Miranda, "Thou think'st there is no more such shapes as he, / Having seen but him and Caliban. Foolish wench" (1.2.481-3)?

65. To what does Ferdinand attribute his weakness? What makes his situation "but light to [him]" (1.2.492)?

66. What motivates Prospero to promise Ariel, "Thou shalt be as free / As mountain winds" (1.2.501-2)?

67. Review the scene: How does Prospero try to guide the meeting of Miranda and Ferdinand? What kind of father is he to Miranda? What kinds of magic or enchantment are working upon Ferdinand?

68. Review the scene and consider the island's hierarchy. Assign a number to each character in the scene with "1" for the most power and "5" for the least.

_____ Miranda

_____ Prospero

_____ Ariel

_____ Caliban

_____ Ferdinand

Jot down the most important lines from which you derive your answer along with some notes about your reasoning. Include notes on what, if anything, makes it difficult to rank any of the characters.

ACT 2, SCENE 1

1. As the scene opens, with what argument does Gonzalo try to convince Alonso to "be merry" (2.1.1-9)?

2. What does Alonso think he has lost that would make it difficult for him to be merry?

3. Sebastian and Antonio interrupt Gonzalo with punning, witty remarks. (A *pun* is the use of a word in a statement that simultaneously suggests two or more meanings of the word and, thus, two or more ways to understand the statement. A speaker can make a pun on a word that has more than one meaning or on a word that sounds like another word.)

    a. Quote one such remark and explain how the pun or witticism works.

    b. What do Sebastian and Antonio's responses show about their attitude toward Gonzalo?

4. What does Sebastian reveal about his attitude toward his brother, King Alonso? Quote one or two of his remarks and derive your answer from them.

5. How does Adrian describe the island (2.1.35, 41, 45)? Quote key phrases.

6. With what quips do Antonio and Sebastian reject his description?

7. What does Gonzalo point out about their garments after the shipwreck (2.1.59-61, 65-7)?

8. From where were the king and his entourage traveling? What were they doing there? (2.1.65-71)?

9. Consult a map, and then roughly sketch one of your own on which you place Milan, Naples, Tunis, Carthage, Argier (Algeria). Where must the island be? Mark its possible location on your map.

10. EXTRA RESEARCH OPPORTUNITY: Gonzalo tells Adrian that "Not since widow Dido's time" was Tunis "graced . . . with such a paragon to their queen" (2.1.70-2).

    a.   Who was Dido? To whom was she married?

    b.   Once a widow, with whom did she fall in love? How did the relationship end?

    c.   In what light does Gonzalo's comparison of Claribel to Dido cast Claribel's recent marriage?

11. What reason does Alonso give for wishing that he "had never / Married [his] daughter" in Tunis (2.1.102-3)?

12. To what does Alonso refer and to whom does he speak when he asks, "What strange fish / Hath made his meal on thee?" (2.1.107-8)?

13. Why, according to Sebastian, may Alonso thank himself for the "great loss" of his son (2.1.118)?

14. What do Sebastian's remarks ("Sir, you may thank yourself . . . The fault's your own" (2.1.118-30)) indicate about his attitude toward his brother, King Alonso?

15. What can you deduce from Sebastian's comments about Claribel's marriage to the King of Tunis? What kind of marriage was this?

16. What prompts Gonzalo to tell Sebastian: "You rub the sore / When you should bring the plaster" (2.1.133-4)? ("Plaster" here means "a small dressing consisting of an absorbent pad attached to a piece of adhesive material, used to cover a superficial wound" (*OED* 1a).)

Analyze Gonzalo's metaphor Gonzalo by sorting its vehicle and tenor.

<u>vehicle</u>   :   <u>tenor</u>

17. Reread Gonzalo's speech starting, "I'the commonwealth I would by contraries / Execute all things" and ending, "I would with such perfection govern, sir, / To excel the Golden Age" (2.1.142-51, 153-8, 161-2).

    a.   How does Gonzalo imagine life on the island?

    b.   What kind of government does he imagine?

    c.   What would men and women do and not do?

    d.   What opportunity does Gonzalo see on this island, which he believes is uninhabited?

18. Sebastian interrupts, "Yet he would be king on't" (2.1.151). What criticism of Gonzalo's idea for the island does Sebastian's quip imply?

19. When Alonso falls asleep, what does Antonio's "strong imagination se[e]" (2.1.202)?

20. How does Antonio describe Claribel and her new home? ("She that is Queen of Tunis.. . . Be rough and razorable" (2.1.240-44).)

21. Antonio says of Claribel:

> She that from whom
> We all were sea-swallowed, though some cast again,
> And by that destiny to perform an act
> Whereof what's past is prologue, what to come
> In yours, and my, discharge. (2.1.244-8)

a. What does Antonio mean when he says that after being "sea-swallowed," some were "cast again"? What does "cast" mean here? Give a synonym or two.

b. Consider Antonio's next phrase, "And by that destiny to *perform an act* / Whereof what's past is *prologue*." From what world do the vehicles of Antonio's language—"perform an act," "prologue"—come?

c. Considering this figurative language, what second meaning does the word "cast" acquire?

d. What "act" is Antonio implying they have been cast to perform?

e. How might Antonio's assertion that "destiny" has "cast" them to "perform" this "act" help to persuade a reluctant Sebastian? What world view does Antonio propose with his choice of language?

22. When Sebastian remembers how Antonio "did supplant [his] brother Prospero" (2.1.265-6), what does Antonio say about having done so? Write down and analyze the metaphor he uses.

23. When Sebastian goes on to ask directly, "But for your conscience," Antonio responds,

> Ay, sir. Where lies that? If 'twere a kibe,
> 'Twould put me to my slipper. But I feel not
> This deity in my bosom. Twenty consciences
> That stand 'twixt me and Milan, candied be they
> And melt ere they molest! (2.1.271-5)

Identify and analyze the metaphors Antonio uses as you explain his response.

24. Draw and label a diagram that explains the relationships among Antonio, Sebastian, Alonso, and Prospero.

25. To whom does Antonio refer as "Sir Prudence" (2.1.281)? What does Antonio suggest he can do to Alonso? And what does Antonio say Sebastian might do to "Sir Prudence"? (Read through to line 291 ("To fall it on Gonzalo") to find the answer.)

26. Who are "all the rest" (2.1.282)? How, according to Antonio will "all the rest" behave once he and Sebastian execute his plan?

27. How does Ariel interrupt Antonio and Sebastian's plan?

28. How do Sebastian and Antonio explain themselves when King Alonso, awakened, asks, "Why are you drawn" (2.1.303)?

29. Review the sequence of events and conversations in the scene. What comments have been made about power and governance? Make a list; include speaker and citation.

30. Review the scene and consider the hierarchy now. Assign a number to each main character in the scene with "1" for the most power and "5" for the least.

_____ Gonzalo

_____ Alonso

_____ Sebastian

_____ Antonio

_____ Ariel

Jot down the most important lines from which you derive your answer along with some notes about your reasoning. Include notes on what, if anything, makes it difficult to rank any of the characters.

ACT 2, SCENE 2

1. What is Caliban doing as the scene opens? How does he describe what Prospero's "spirits" do to him (2.2.3)?

2. When Trinculo enters, what does Caliban think he is?

3. What does Caliban decide to do upon seeing Trinculo? What makes him decide to do so?

4. Reread Trinculo's speech upon discovering Caliban ("What have we here . . . that hath lately suffered by a thunderbolt" (2.2.24-35)). Notice Trinculo's clowning as you consider what the scene reveals about encounters between strangers.

   a. When Trinculo sees Caliban, he asks, "What have we here? A man or a fish? Dead or alive?" (2.2.24). What, at first, does Trinculo decide Caliban is? Quote the phrase.

   b. Explain Trinculo's comment: "Were I in England now . . . and had but this fish painted, not a holiday fool there but would give a piece of silver. There would this monster make a man" (2.2.27-9). How, in Trinculo's view, would "this monster" (Caliban) "make a man" in England? Think of two ways to understand the word "make," and then propose two ways to understand the line.

c. "When they will not give a doit to relieve a lame beggar, they will lay out ten to see a dead Indian" (2.2.30-1): Of what does Trinculo accuse the people in England?

d. "Legged like a man, and his fins like arms" (2.2.32): What does Trinculo say now about this "fish"? What else might you conclude if you were to notice that a creature you earlier had decided was a "strange fish" (2.2.26) is "legged" and has "fins like arms"?

e. Indeed, Trinculo eventually decides "this is not fish, but an islander" (2.2.34). What does this ridiculous scene suggest about why Trinculo takes so long to arrive at this decision?

5. Note that Stephano finds "comfort" (2.2.43, 54) in his bottle. What does this suggest about the state he is in when he comments on Trinculo and Caliban, who are underneath Caliban's gabardine?

6. What does Stephano plan to do with the "monster of the isle with four legs" (2.2.62) if he can "recover him, and keep him tame" (2.2.65)?

7. What does Caliban think Stephano is (2.2.68, 2.2.75-6)?

8. What does Caliban beg and promise Stephano (2.2.68-9, 2.2.75-6)? What do Caliban's comments here show about his experience on the island? About his relationship with Prospero?

9. What does Stephano do for the "monster" who, he thinks, is shaking with "ague" (2.2.62-3)? (*Ague* means "an acute or high fever" (*OED* 1).)

10. Consider the possibilities for comedy (2.2.84-8) about the "delicate monster" with the "two voices." If you were directing the play, how would you direct the actors here?

11. Why does Trinculo "hope" Stephano is "not drowned" (2.2.102-3)? What does Trinculo imply he would think about the figure he is seeing if Stephano had drowned?

12. How does Trinculo refer to Caliban now (2.2.103)?

13. Why does Caliban decide to "kneel" to Stephano (2.2.109)? Upon what object does Caliban swear to be his "true subject" (2.2.115)? What does this oath imply about Caliban's subjecting himself to Stephano?

14. What prompts Trinculo to call Caliban "A most poor credulous monster" (2.2.136)?

15. Reread Caliban's speech:

    I'll show thee the best springs. I'll pluck thee berries.
    I'll fish for thee, and get thee wood enough.
    A plague upon the tyrant that I serve,
    I'll bear him no more sticks, but follow thee,
    Thou wondrous man. (2.2.150-4)

    a. Caliban promises to work for Stephano, including "to get [him] wood enough." For whom have we seen Caliban do such work? Under what conditions?

    b. What prompts Caliban to promise to do such labor for Stephano when he will "bear [Prospero] no more sticks"?

16. Reread what Caliban promises Stephano ("I prithee let me bring thee . . . Wilt thou go with me?" 2.2.157-62)). How does this promise compare to Caliban's claim about his early encounters with Prospero? (Reread: "And then I loved thee, . . . and fertile" (1.2.337-9)).

17. Consider Caliban's plan: what is the cost of Caliban's freeing himself from his "tyrant" Prospero (2.2.152)?

18. Considering what he has just offered to do for Stephano, what do you think about Caliban's song about "Freedom, high-day" (2.2.169-76)?

19. Compare the way Antonio frees himself from being subject to his king, Prospero, to the way Caliban frees himself from being subject to his master, Prospero. (Consider what each offers to free himself from being Prospero's subject.)

20. Review the scene and consider the hierarchy. Assign a number to each character in the scene with "1" for the most power and "3" for the least.

_____ Caliban

_____ Trinculo

_____ Stephano

Jot down the most important lines from which you derive your answer along with some notes about your reasoning. Include notes on what, if anything, makes it difficult to rank any of the characters.

21. Look back at Ferdinand and Miranda's encounter with each other and compare it to Trinculo and Stephano's encounter with Caliban. What does each character think the stranger is? What surprises each character about the stranger? Listen for verbal echoes. Consider, for instance, the repetition of the word *wonder*.

22. Consider possible influences (including alcohol, the shipwreck, and prior beliefs) on the various characters' perceptions of the stranger(s) he or she encounters. Jot down some of your observations about what shapes each character's perceptions. Quote and cite key lines.

Miranda's:

Ferdinand's:

Caliban's:

Trinculo's:

Stephano's:

ACT 3, SCENE 1

1. As the scene opens, what is Ferdinand doing? Why? Who has done this job before?

2. How does Ferdinand feel about his work? What makes him feel this way?

3. What makes Miranda feel that Ferdinand can rest for three hours? Is she correct about Prospero's whereabouts?

4. When Ferdinand refuses to rest, what does Miranda offer?

5. By what, according to Prospero, is Miranda "infected" (3.1.31)? What is the effect of Prospero's choice of word? (Look up *infected* in the *Oxford English Dictionary*.)

6. What had Prospero forbidden Miranda to do (3.1.37)?

7. *Miranda* in Latin means "worthy of admiration or wonder." How might this etymology add to our understanding of how the name functions in this scene?

8. Ferdinand tells Miranda of other ladies he has "eyed": "many a time / The harmony of their tongues hath into bondage / Brought my too diligent ear" (3.1.40-2). What does Ferdinand's image suggest about the dangers of speech and of listening? What does he suggest, metaphorically, that a tongue can do to an ear?

9. How does Miranda respond to Ferdinand's flattering comparison of her to other women?

10. What does Miranda say is the "jewel in her dower" (3.1.54)? Explain her metaphor.

11. What makes Ferdinand add, "I do think a king" after referring to himself as a "prince" (3.1.60)? What would make him add, "I would not so" (3.1.61)? (*Would* here means "wish.")

12. Why, according to Ferdinand, is he "this patient log-man" (3.1.67)?

13. What is Prospero's response to Miranda and Ferdinand's declaration of love (3.1.74-6)? Considering this declaration, what might motivate Prospero's treatment of Ferdinand?

14. What does Miranda offer Ferdinand?

15. Note Ferdinand's response: "Ay, with a heart as willing / As bondage e'er of freedom" (3.1.88-9).

    a. What is the premise about bondage and freedom contained in Ferdinand's statement? What does Ferdinand imply bondage is "e'er" (*ever*) willing to do or have?

    b. Explain how Ferdinand uses his premise about the relationship between bondage and freedom to describe the willingness of his heart.

    c. What does this response add to Ferdinand's previous comments about slavery?

16. Prospero comments, "So glad of this as they I cannot be" (3.1.92):

  a. To what does "this" refer?

  b. Why can't Prospero be "So glad of this as they"? Give two possible reasons.

17. Review the scene and consider the hierarchy. Assign a number to each character in the scene with "1" for the most power and "3" for the least.

  _____ Ferdinand

  _____ Miranda

  _____ Prospero

  Jot down the most important lines from which you derive your answer along with some notes about your reasoning. Include notes on what, if anything, makes it difficult to rank any of the characters.

ACT 3, SCENE 2

1. As the scene opens, what do Stephano and Trinculo call Caliban?

2. What does Trinculo call Caliban after Caliban refuses to serve him (3.2.24-7)?   What had he previously decided Caliban was?

3. When Caliban addresses Stephano as "my lord," Trinculo wonders, "That a monster should be such a natural" (3.2.29-30).

    a. Some editors explain the meaning of *natural* here as "half-wit." Explain Trinculo's comment if we take *natural* to mean "A person having a low learning ability or intellectual capacity; a person born with impaired intelligence" (*OED* II 7).

    b. Then, look up *natural* in the *Oxford English Dictionary*, note another possible meaning of the word, and propose another possible meaning of Trinculo's remark.

4. What does Caliban say about Prospero (3.2.39-41)? How, according to Caliban, did Prospero get the island (3.2.39-41, 49-50)?

5. Referring to specific lines of the play, explain how the Yale edition's editor arrived at the stage directions "*(to Trinculo)*" before Caliban says, "Thou liest, thou jesting monkey, thou" (3.2.42).

6. Note the stage direction, "Enter Ariel, Invisible." How would you direct the scene to make Ariel "invisible"?

7. What does the invisible Ariel accomplish by saying, "Thou liest" (3.2.41)? What happens as a result?

8. What makes Stephano beat Trinculo? ("Take thou that" (3.2.71).) How does Caliban respond?

9. What does Caliban plot? What does Caliban stress that Stephano must seize in order to accomplish the plot?

10. Do you agree with Caliban that all the spirits Prospero commands hate him (3.2.90-1)? Quote and cite the lines from which you derive your answer.

11. Why must Caliban rely on Prospero's assessment of "The beauty of [Prospero's] daughter" (3.2.95)? What earlier situation does this echo?

12. Why might Caliban tell Stephano that Miranda would "become [his] bed" (3.2.101)? (Remember Caliban's thwarted attempt to "peopl[e] . . . the isle with Calibans" (1.2.351-2).)

13. What prompts Stephano to say, "If thou beest a man, show thyself in thy likeness" and Trinculo to exclaim, "O forgive me my sins!" (3.2.125-7)?

14. How does Caliban reassure Stephano and Trinculo? How does he describe the island?

15. Notice that Caliban speaks in verse whereas Trinculo and Stephano speak in prose. *(For explanations of* verse *and* prose, *see pages 75-6 of appendix 1, "Listening for Meter.")* What does this difference add to our understanding of Caliban?

16. As the scene ends, who is following whom?

17. Review the scene and assign a number to each character— "1" for the most power and "4" for the least.

   _____ Stephano

   _____ Trinculo

   _____ Caliban

   _____ Ariel

   Jot down the most important lines from which you derive your answer along with some notes about your reasoning. Include notes on what, if anything, makes it difficult to rank any of the characters.

ACT 3, SCENE 3

1. Whom have Gonzalo and Alonso "stray[ed] to find" (3.3.9)? What makes them call off the search?

2. Of what does Antonio remind Sebastian (3.3.11-13)? How does Sebastian respond?

3. What, according to the stage direction, do "several strange shapes" do? Who is looking on as they do so?

4. Upon the appearance of these shapes:

   a. What is Sebastian now willing to believe?

   b. What is Antonio now willing to believe?

   c. What does Gonzalo wonder?

5. How does Gonzalo respond to Alonso's refusal to eat the banquet left behind by the shapes?

6. What is a *harpy*? What does Ariel's appearance as a harpy add to the banquet's vanishing?

7. Reread Ariel's speech ("You are three men of sin . . . And a clear life ensuing" (3.3.53-82)):

    a. For what does Ariel say "Destiny" is responsible?

    b. Explain Ariel's claim that he and his "fellows" are "ministers of fate" (3.3.60-1).

    c. Consider what Ariel says and then write a stage direction for what happens when Alonso and his men draw their swords.

    d. What, according to Ariel, hath the sea "requit" (3.3.71)?

    e. What does Ariel say will happen to them on the isle?

8. What does Prospero say to Ariel about the banquet? How does he treat Ariel now?

9. How does Prospero refer to Ferdinand and Miranda now (3.3.91-3)?

10. What does Alonso think the billows spoke, the winds sang, and the thunder pronounced (3.3.95-9)?

11. Explain Alonso's logic when he says, "Therefore my son i'th'ooze is bedded" (3.3.100).

12. Consider Gonzalo's comment: "Their great guilt, / Like poison given to work a great time after, / Now 'gins to bite the spirits" (3.3.104-6).

    a. For what does Gonzalo think they feel guilty?

    b. Analyze Gonzalo's simile ("guilt / Like poison given to work a great time after").

       vehicle   :   tenor

47

c. What does the simile imply he suspects "this ecstasy / May now provoke them to" (3.3.108-9)?

13. Review the scene and assign a number to each main character— "1" for the most power and "6" for the least.

_____ Gonzalo

_____ Alonso

_____ Antonio

_____ Sebastian

_____ Prospero

_____ Ariel

Jot down the most important lines from which you derive your answer along with some notes about your reasoning. Include notes on what, if anything, makes it difficult to rank any of the characters.

ACT 4, SCENE 1

1. Reread Prospero's comment to Ferdinand that opens the scene:

    > If I have too austerely punished you,
    > Your compensation makes amends, for I
    > Have given you a third of mine own life,
    > Or that for which I live, who once again
    > I tender to thy hand. (4.1.1-5)

    And reread Prospero's later comment:

    > Then, as my gift and thine own acquisition
    > Worthily purchased, take my daughter. (4.1.13-14)

    a. With what kind of language does Prospero refer to his daughter's pending marriage? List four key words.

    b. What does this language show about Prospero's view of marriage?

    c. How might Miranda be "a third of [Prospero's] own life"? Give two possibilities.

2. What "test" does Prospero think Ferdinand has "strangely stood" (4.1.7)? How has Ferdinand done so?

3. With what does Prospero threaten Ferdinand if he "do[th] break [Miranda's] virgin knot before / All sanctimonious ceremonies may / With full and holy rite be ministered" (4.1.15-17)?

4. How does Ferdinand respond to Prospero's threat?

5. What does Miranda say during this conversation about her marriage?

6. What does Prospero order Ariel to do? To whom might Prospero refer as the "rabble" over whom he gives Ariel "power" (4.1.37-8)?

7. Prospero warns Ferdinand to be "true," not to "give dalliance / Too much the rein," and to "Be more abstemious" (4.1.51-3). What might prompt Prospero's remarks? What might be happening while Prospero speaks to Ariel? Write a stage direction for Ferdinand and Miranda.

8. "The strongest oaths are straw / To th'fire i'the blood" (4.1.53). Sort the metaphor's vehicle and tenor:

vehicle   :   tenor

What does Prospero's metaphor imply about the strength of oaths?

9. With what metaphor does Ferdinand respond to Prospero's warning?

10. Who is Iris? (Consult your editor's notes or a mythology reference book.)

11. Who is Ceres? (Consult your editor's notes or a mythology reference book.)

12. Why, according to Iris, has Ceres's "queen / Summoned [Ceres] hither to this short-grassed green" (4.1.82-3)?

13. Who is Juno? (Consult your editor's notes or a mythology reference book.)

14. Juno to Ceres: "How does my bounteous sister? Go with me / To bless this twain, that they may prosperous be, / And honored in their issue" (4.1.103-5). Explain the blessing Juno plans for Ferdinand and Miranda. (Consult your editors' notes or a dictionary, and be sure to explain the words *twain*, *prosperous*, and *issue*.)

15. How does Ceres's blessing (4.1.110-17) connect the bounty of the earth to Ferdinand and Miranda's marriage?

16. Why might Ferdinand ask, "May I be bold / To think these spirits" (4.1.119-20)? Why would he think it "bold"? (Who else had he thought was a spirit?)

17. For what does Ferdinand wish (4.1.122-4)?

18. What makes Prospero suddenly dismiss the spirits and stop the pageant?

19. Reread Prospero's speech to Ferdinand:

> Our revels now are ended. These our actors
> (As I foretold you) were all spirits and
> Are melted into air, into thin air,
> And like the baseless fabric of this vision
> The cloud-capped towers, the gorgeous palaces,
> The solemn temples, the great globe itself,
> Yes, all which it inherit, shall dissolve
> And like this insubstantial pageant faded
> Leave not a rack behind. We are such stuff
> As dreams are made on, and our little life
> Is rounded with a sleep. (4.1.148-58)

a. What does Prospero say about the "actors" of the pageant they have just seen?

b. To what does Prospero refer as "this vision"?

c. What does Prospero assert when he says that "The cloud-capped towers, the gorgeous palaces, / The solemn temples, the great globe itself" are "like the baseless fabric of this vision"? What, according to Prospero, will happen to the towers, palaces, temples, and globe? What shall be left behind?

d. How is "our little life . . . rounded with a sleep"? What kind of "sleep"?

e. Do you agree with Prospero that an insubstantial pageant, such as a play, "Leave[s] not a rack behind"? Explain why or why not. (A *rack* is "A bank of cloud, fog, or mist; a wisp of cloud or vapour" (*OED* 2b).)

f. To what "stuff" might Prospero refer in his phrase "such stuff / As dreams are made on"?

g. If we are "such stuff / As dreams are made on," what does Prospero imply "our little life" will leave behind? Do you agree with Prospero's idea? Explain why or why not.

h. Note that the theater of Shakespeare's company was called The Globe. What extra meaning, then, does the phrase "the great globe" take on in Prospero's speech? Was anything left behind after The Globe Theater was closed and eventually torn down in the mid-1600s?

20. Where has Ariel left Caliban, Trinculo, and Stephano?

21. Reread Prospero's comment about Caliban:

A devil, a born devil, on whose nature
Nurture can never stick. On whom my pains,
Humanely taken, all, all lost, quite lost,
And, as with age, his body uglier grows,
So his mind cankers. (4.1.188-92)

a. What conclusion does Prospero draw from his knowledge of Caliban's plot against him? Explain, in your answer, what Prospero means when he claims that "Nurture can never stick" on Caliban's "nature."

b. To what might Prospero refer with "my pains / Humanely taken"? What pains has Prospero taken on Caliban? Give two possibilities with references to the text.

c. What other than Caliban's being a "born devil" might account for his plot against Prospero? (Again, refer specifically to the text.)

d. Analyze the metaphor, "his mind cankers." Then explain what Prospero asserts here about Caliban's mind.

22. For what purpose does Prospero direct Ariel to bring the "trumpery" from his house to "hang them on this line" (4.1.186, 193)?

23. What are Trinculo and Stephano concerned about having lost?

24. What distracts Trinculo and Stephano from the plot of murdering Prospero? How does Caliban respond to their distraction?

25. What chases Caliban, Stephano, and Trinculo?

26. What does Prospero promise Ariel that he shall have "shortly" (4.1.263-4)?

27. How might Ariel feel about this promise? Give your reason(s).

28. Review the two parts of this scene and assign a number to the main characters in each part— "1" for the most power and "5" for the least.

4.1.1-163	4.1.163-265
_____ Prospero	_____ Prospero
_____ Ferdinand	_____ Ariel
_____ Miranda	_____ Caliban
_____ Ariel	_____ Stephano
_____ Iris, Juno, Ceres	_____ Trinculo

Jot down the most important lines from which you derive your answers along with some notes about your reasoning. Include notes on what, if anything, makes it difficult to rank any of the characters.

ACT 5, SCENE 1

1. How does Ariel respond when Prospero asks the time ("How's the day?" (5.1.3))? Of what does he remind Prospero?

2. What time was it at the beginning of the play? (Look back at 1.2.239-40.) During what amount of time have the actions of the play occurred?

3. Ariel tells Prospero that his "affections / Would become tender" if he were to behold the grieving King and his followers. How does Ariel respond to Prospero's asking, "Dost thou think so, spirit" (5.1.18-19)? Quote Ariel's answer.

4. Reread Prospero's response to Ariel's report:

    Hast thou (which art but air) a touch, a feeling
    Of their afflictions, and shall not myself,
    One of their kind, that relish all as sharply,
    Passion as they, be kindlier moved than thou art?
    Though with their high wrongs I am struck to th' quick,
    Yet, with my nobler reason, 'gainst my fury
    Do I take part. The rarer action is
    In virtue than in vengeance. They, being penitent,
    The sole drift of my purpose doth extend
    Not a frown further. (5.1.21-30)

    a. What prompts Prospero to question not being moved by the "afflictions" of the king and his followers?

b. Define "kind" and "kindlier" as Prospero uses each word.

c. What does Prospero imply follows from being "One of their kind"?

d. Do events in the play uphold or contradict this notion? Explain how.

e. What does Prospero say works against his "fury"? Quote the phrase.

f. What reason does Prospero give for not extending his purpose "a frown further"?

5. Reread Prospero's speech that starts, "Ye elves of hills . . ." (5.1.33-57).

a. To whom does Prospero speak?

b. What acts does he claim he has accomplished "By [his] so potent art" (5.1.50)? List a few.

c. What does Prospero announce when he says, "But this rough magic / I here abjure" (5.1.50-1)? *Abjure* means "to renounce or disavow (a thing)" (*OED* 2).

d. Why might Prospero decide to abjure this magic now?

e. What does Prospero pledge to do with his staff? With his book?

6. Prospero describes with a simile how "the charm dissolves":

And as the morning steals upon the night
(Melting the darkness) so their rising sense
Begin to chase the ignorant fumes that mantle
Their clear reason. (5.1.65-8)

a. Sort the simile's vehicle and tenor. (Doing so is a tricky because the tenor also contains metaphoric language.)

vehicle   :   tenor

b. Consider just the vehicle for a moment. What causes morning to "stea[l] upon night"?

c. What, then, does the simile imply about sense's relationship to ignorance?

7. "Mine eyes, ev'n sociable to the show of thine, / Fall fellowly drops" (5.1.63-4): What happens to Prospero when he sees the weeping Gonzalo? What does Prospero say to Gonzalo?

8. What does Prospero say to Alonso?

9. What does he say to Sebastian?

10. What does he say to his brother, Antonio?

11. In what sense would Prospero find Antonio "unnatural"?

12. Analyze the metaphor: "Their understanding / Begins to swell, and the approaching tide / Will shortly fill the reasonable shores / That now lie foul and muddy" (5.1.79-82). Sort its vehicle and tenor.

vehicle : tenor

What does Prospero's metaphor imply about understanding and reason?

13. What prompts Prospero to ask Ariel to fetch his "hat and rapier" (5.1.84)?

14. After Prospero tells Ariel, "I shall miss thee," what does Prospero promise him (5.1.95-6)?

15. What does Prospero order Ariel to do?

16. How does Alonso respond when Prospero announces himself, "The wrongèd Duke of Milan" (5.1.107)?

17. What "tales" could Prospero tell about Sebastian and Antonio, whom he calls "my brace of lords," (5.1.126-9)? What might motivate Prospero not to tell this tale?

18. What does Prospero say to his brother, Antonio (5.1.30-4)?

19. Note that Antonio says nothing in response. How would you direct this interaction between the brothers? How might Antonio respond nonverbally? Write a stage direction for Antonio.

20. Why does Prospero tell Alonso that he has lost a daughter in the tempest? In what sense would Prospero feel he has lost Miranda?

21. How does Alonso respond to Prospero's claim?

22. Note Prospero's description of his arrival on the island: "know for certain / That I am Prospero, and that very duke / Which was thrust forth of Milan, who most strangely / Upon this shore, where you were wracked, was landed / To be the lord on't" (5.1.158-62). What is Prospero's view of how he came to be "lord" of the island?

23. "My dukedom since you have given me again, / I will requite you with as good a thing" (5.1.168-9): With what "thing" will Prospero requite Alonso for his dukedom?

24. Miranda and Ferdinand are "playing chess" in the cell. Describe the object of the game of chess, and then comment on what Miranda and Ferdinand's playing chess adds to the scene.

25. Of what does Miranda accuse Ferdinand? What might motivate her to "call it fair play" (5.1.172-4)?

26. Upon seeing Ferdinand, why does Alonso fear he might "twice lose" his "dear son" (5.1.175-7)?

27. What prompts Miranda to say, "O, brave new world, / That has such people in 't" (5.1.183-4)? How would you feel if you were Ferdinand and heard this remark?

28. Note Ferdinand's response to his father's wondering if Miranda is a goddess: "Sir, she is mortal, / But by immortal Providence, she's mine" (5.1.188-9). How might Ferdinand think that Miranda is his by "immortal Providence"?

29. Explain what Alonso means when he asks, "how oddly will it sound that I / Must ask my child forgiveness?" (5.1.197-8). To whom does Alonso refer as "my child"? For what does he feel he must he ask forgiveness?

30. Why might Prospero "stop" Alonso from asking for forgiveness?

31. What does Gonzalo ask the gods to do? What does he think the gods have done (5.1.201-4)?

32. What is the effect of Ferdinand and Miranda's marriage on Prospero and on those from Milan and Naples responsible for Prospero's exile? Quote and cite the lines from which you derive your answer.

33. What does the Boatswain report about the ship?

34. Ariel announces, "Sir, all this service / Have I done since I went" (5.1.226-7). Why might the editor have added the stage direction that this is *aside to Prospero*? How else might Ariel and Prospero's interaction be directed? Write a stage direction, and then explain the effect of the alternate staging.

35. How does Prospero describe Caliban's mother? What does he say about her powers (5.1.271-4)?

36. To what does Prospero refer when he says, "This thing of darkness I / Acknowledge mine" (5.1.278-9)? What "thing"? What kind of "darkness"?

37. What does Caliban fear will happen to him?

38. How does Prospero respond to Alonso's calling Caliban a "strange thing" (5.1.292)? What, if anything, does this tell us about Caliban? About Alonso and Prospero? Give two possibilities.

39. What does Prospero order Caliban to do (5.1.294-6)?

40. What does Caliban say about his recent "worship" of Stephano (5.1.298-300)?

41. How does Sebastian add to Alonso's order that Stephano and Trinculo "bestow [their] luggage where they found it" (5.1.301-2)? What is Sebastian unwilling to do for the wrong-doers that Alonso is willing to do? What, especially considering Sebastian's recent thwarted plot, does this reveal about Sebastian's character?

42. What is Prospero's plan for the night? For the morning?

43. Prospero promises Alonso "calm seas, auspicious gales, / And sail, so expeditious, that shall catch / Your royal fleet far off" (5.1.317-9). What does he then tell Ariel?

44. Why would Prospero tell his guests, "Please you draw near" (5.1.321)?

45. Review the scene, and think about who has power over whom now. How have hierarchies shifted? Jot down important lines and some notes about what they indicate. Include notes on what, if anything, makes it difficult to decide which characters have more power than others.

EPILOGUE

1. If Prospero, alone on stage now, speaks the epilogue, to whom is it addressed?

2. "Now my charms are all o'erthrown, / And what strength I have's mine own. / Which is most faint" (Epi. 1-3).

    a. What "charms" of Prospero's have been overthrown? How?

    b. If, as Prospero asserts, the faint strength he now has is his own, what does he imply about his former strength?

3. "I must be here confined by you, / Or sent to Naples" (Epi. 4-5): Who is "you"? Where is "here"?

4. "But release me from my bands / With the help of your good hands" (Epi. 9-10). What can "good hands" do to release Prospero from his bands?

5. What, then, would be the "spell" that would confine Prospero to "this bare island" (Epi. 8)?

6. Who now, according to Prospero, has the power to cast spells? What does Prospero imply about how his role has changed?

7. "Gentle breath of yours, my sails / Must fill, or else my project fails, / Which was to please" (Epi. 11-13):

   a. To what does Prospero refer when he says "gentle breath of yours"?

   b. In what way could such breath fill his sails?

   c. What does Prospero say was his "project"?

8. Now that Prospero "want[s] / Spirits to enforce, art to enchant," he says his "ending is despair" (Epi. 14-5). (Note that *wants* here means "lacks.") What does he say would "relieve" him of this despair?

9. What does Prospero imply is the reason to pardon another?

10. Prospero says that the audience's "indulgence" (or pardon) will "set [him] free" (Epi. 20). From what will Prospero be set free? How is he confined?

11. Reread the last words Prospero speaks to Ariel (5.1.320-1). How does Prospero's final request (in the epilogue) echo his final remark to Ariel? How has Prospero's role changed?

12. The Epilogue draws an extended comparison between Prospero, the Duke of Milan, on the island and Prospero, an actor, on the stage. You may find that the comparison does not work out neatly. Try, nonetheless, to think through this tricky comparison by charting its elements as best you can.

Prospero : actor (playing Prospero)

charms : _____

bare island : _____

_____ : "you" (audience member)

_____ : gentle breath

sail : _____

Naples : _____

13. Prospero wants to be "sent to Naples."

    a.   To what role will Prospero be restored there?

    b.   What role would Prospero have if he remained confined on the island?

    c.   Explain the parallel, as the play ends, between Prospero and the actor playing Prospero. Where does the actor wish to go? To what role will he be restored there? By what is the actor confined?

14. What does Prospero's speech suggest about theater? About actor and audience?

15. Scan a few lines of the epilogue and note its rhyme scheme. *(See appendix 1, "Listening for Meter.")*

    a. What do you notice about the meter and rhyme scheme of the epilogue?

    b. What does the epilogue's meter and rhyme scheme make it sound like? (How does it compare to the speeches of unrhymed iambic pentameter?)

    c. What does the epilogue's meter and rhyme scheme add to its meaning?

16. Review the epilogue and assign a number to Prospero and to the audience— "1" for the most power and "2" for the least.

_____ Prospero

_____ audience

Jot down the most important phrases from which you derive your answer along with some notes about your reasoning. Include notes on what, if anything, makes it difficult to rank them.

APPENDIX 1. LISTENING FOR METER—AN INTRODUCTION

Actors have long observed that Shakespeare's plays convey their meanings not only through the sense of his language but also through its sounds, including rhyme, alliteration (repeated consonant sounds), and assonance (repeated vowel sounds). Read aloud and consider how the sounds of a speech contribute to its meanings.

This section will help you get started listening for the rhythms of a Shakespeare play by introducing you to meters you will encounter in *The Tempest*.

🗨 For most English literature, **METER** refers to a deliberate pattern of stressed and unstressed syllables.

"Stressed" syllables are the syllables that get the most emphasis when a word or sentence is spoken aloud. (In the literature of some other languages, including Greek and Latin, meter is measured by the length rather than the stress of syllables.)

Keep in mind that you can hear the meter in which a poet has composed a speech or poem even while you can hear how the poet has, at times, varied that meter.

🗨 In a Shakespeare play, speeches in **VERSE** are composed with a repeating pattern of stressed and unstressed syllables and are divided into deliberate lines. Verse is composed in meter.

🗨 In a Shakespeare play, speeches in **PROSE** are composed without a repeating pattern of stressed and unstressed syllables and are not divided into deliberate lines. Prose is not composed in meter.

Examples of VERSE in *The Tempest*:

> *Caliban*   As wicked dew, as e'er my mother brushed
>   With raven's feather from unwholesome fen
>   Drop on you both! A south-west blow on ye,
>   And blister you all o'er! (1.2.322-5)

> *Iris*   Thy turfy mountains, where live nibbling sheep,
>   And flat meads thatched with stover, them to keep— (4.1.62-3)

🗨 *Iris's speech above, two lines that have the same meter and that rhyme, is called a* **COUPLET**.

- When you are reading verse, you will see that the first word of each new line of a speech is capitalized whether or not it begins a new sentence.

- Whatever the size of a book's pages, printers retain the lines of a speech in verse. Thus, often you will see empty space between the end of a line and the right margin of your book's page. If a line of verse is longer than what fits on a particular page, then what remains of the verse line usually is indented and printed directly below.

- When you quote verse, you should retain the capital letters and indicate the line breaks with a forward slash, called a *virgule*. Example: Cursing Prospero, Caliban calls, "A south-west blow on ye, / And blister you all o'er!" (1.2.324-5).

An example of PROSE in *The Tempest*:

> *Stephano*   This is some monster of the isle with four legs, who
> hath got (as I take it) an ague.   Where the devil should
> he learn our language? (2.2.62-4)

- When you are reading prose, you will see that lines are printed until a word nearly reaches the right margin of the page. The first word of a new line, which varies depending on the size of the book, is not capitalized unless it happens to begin a new sentence.

❧ An **IAMB** is a poetic foot of one unstressed syllable (marked "˘") followed by one stressed syllable (marked "/"). Examples of single words that are iambs are:

$$\overset{\textstyle\smile\quad /}{\text{against}} \qquad\qquad \overset{\textstyle\smile\quad /}{\text{enchant}}$$

❧ **IAMBIC PENTAMETER** names the meter of a line of verse with five ("penta") iambs. An example:

$$\overset{\textstyle\smile\;\;/\;\;\smile\;\;/\;\;\smile\;\;/\;\;\smile\;\;/\;\;\smile\;\;/}{\text{The very minute bids thee ope thine ear.}} \quad (1.2.37)$$

❧ Marking the stressed and unstressed syllables of a line of verse in the manner above is called **SCANSION**. To **SCAN** a line of verse is to listen for and mark its stressed and unstressed syllables and to notice what kind and how many of the repeating foot make up the line. Scansion also includes noticing any variations in the meter of a line. *(See pages 77-8 for examples of variations in iambic pentameter).*

🍂 A **TROCHEE** is a poetic foot of one stressed syllable followed by one unstressed syllable. Examples of single words that are trochees are:

/ ˘
nothing

/ ˘
suffer

🍂 **TROCHAIC TETRAMETER** names the meter of a line with four ("tetra") trochees. Examples:

/ ˘ / ˘ / ˘ / ˘
Vines with clust'ring bunches growing,
/ ˘ / ˘ / ˘ / ˘
Plants with goodly burden bowing, (4.1.112-13)

🍂 *The above lines are another example of a COUPLET—two rhyming lines with the same meter.*

/ ˘ / ˘ / ˘ /
Of his bones are coral made.
/ ˘ / ˘ / ˘ /
Those are pearls that were his eyes, (1.2.399-400)

🍂 *The meter of these lines, which lack the unstressed syllable of their final trochee, is named* **CATALECTIC TROCHAIC TETRAMETER**.

Although much of *The Tempest* is composed in iambic pentameter, you will hear many variations in the meter. Below are a few to listen for. When you notice a variation, consider what it adds to a speech's meanings.

🍂 Some iambic lines end with an extra unstressed syllable. Such a line is said to have a **FEMININE ENDING**. An example:

˘ / ˘ / ˘ / ˘ / ˘ / ˘
This island's mine by Sycorax my mother, (1.2.332)

🍂 Some iambic lines substitute a trochee for one of the iambs. Here's an example of an iambic pentameter line that begins with a **TROCHEE SUBSTITUTION**:

/ ˘ ˘ / ˘ / ˘ / ˘ /
Worthy Sebastian? O, what might? No more. (2.1.199)

77

✍ Some iambic lines omit the unstressed syllable of the first iamb. Such a line is called **HEADLESS IAMBIC PENTAMETER**. An example:

/ ˘ / ˘ / ˘ / ˘ /
Twelve year since, Miranda, twelve year since, (1.2.53)

You may be wondering why this line is considered headless iambic pentameter *rather than catalectic trochaic pentameter. The way we hear the rhythm of a particular line depends on the rhythm of the lines that surround it. If you look at your text, you will see that in this case the surrounding lines are iambic, which leads us to hear this line as* headless iambic pentameter.

Sometimes a line of verse is spoken by more than one character. Here is a single iambic pentameter line shared by Prospero and Miranda:

Prospero	˘ / ˘ / There's no harm done.
Miranda	˘ / ˘ / O woe the day!
Prospero	˘ / No harm. (1.2.14)

And here is a single iambic pentameter line shared by Prospero and Ariel:

Prospero	˘ / ˘ / ˘ / What is't thou canst demand?
Ariel	˘ / ˘ / My liberty. (1.2.245)

Note that the contraction of "is it" as "is't" becomes one stressed syllable and keeps the meter of the line.

APPENDIX 2. READING FIGURATIVE LANGUAGE—
AN INTRODUCTION TO METAPHOR, SIMILE, METONYMY, & SYNECDOCHE

Shakespeare's plays are famous for their figures of speech, which are rich in meaning and sometimes difficult to understand. What follows is an introduction to four key figures of speech—metaphor, simile, metonymy, and synecdoche—along with some techniques you can use as you work to understand them.

> ✍ A **METAPHOR** asserts that one thing is another thing and demands that we imagine how it can be so.
>
> "A rose is a flower" is not a metaphor. A rose is **LITERALLY** a flower. Anyone could find this out by looking up "rose" in a dictionary.
>
> "Love is a rose" is a metaphor because it demands that we imagine how love is like a rose. A metaphor can be understood as true only if taken **FIGURATIVELY**.

Our English word *metaphor* is borrowed from Greek. "*Meta*" means *trans-* or *across*, and "*phor*" means *port* or *carry*; thus, *metaphor* can be translated as *transport*. The metaphor above transports a *rose* from the world of gardening to explain something in the world of emotions, namely, *love.* Metaphors explain something in one world by transporting something from a distant world for comparison.

One way to analyze a metaphor is to sort its TENOR and VEHICLE, terms coined by I. A. Richards in his 1936 book *The Philosophy of Rhetoric.*

> ✍ The **TENOR** is the subject of the metaphor—what the speaker is talking about.
>
> ✍ The **VEHICLE** is what is transported for comparison to illuminate some quality of the tenor.
>
> In the metaphor "love is a rose," *love* is the tenor and *rose* is the vehicle.

The combination of a metaphor's vehicle and tenor prompts you to recognize that you're hearing or reading a metaphor because the statement would be otherwise absurd or impossible. As Richards emphasizes, the interaction of the tenor and the vehicle produces the metaphor's meaning.

79

Take, for example, the opening of Shakespeare's Sonnet 68:

> Thus is his cheek the map of days outworn,

When we read this line, we realize that a literal cheek cannot also be a literal map, and so we know that we're reading a metaphor. Here *cheek* is the tenor—what the speaker is talking about—and *map* is the vehicle—what the speaker has transported from the world of diagrams, paper, and ink to describe "cheek" by comparison.

Sometimes it is helpful to sort the metaphor's vehicle and tenor in a chart:

vehicle	:	tenor
map	:	cheek

And sometimes it is helpful to sketch the metaphor, trying to show both its vehicle (cheek) and its tenor (map). Here is an example:

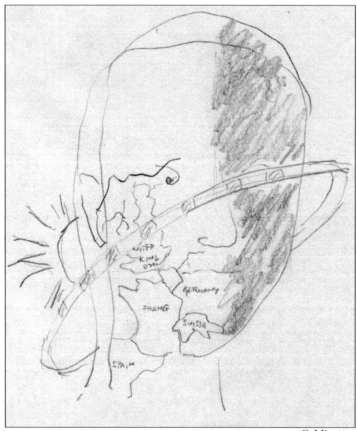

G. Minette

✍ A **SIMILE** asserts that one thing is "like" or "as" another thing and demands that we imagine how.

"Lucinda is like her grandmother" is not a simile. It is a **LITERAL** statement.

"Lucinda is like a hurricane" is a simile. It is a **FIGURATIVE** statement.

Of course we may have to figure out how Lucinda is like her grandmother, but comparing Lucinda and her grandmother—who both are human, female, and kin—doesn't demand that we use our imagination to find similarities in altogether different categories of things as we must if we are to understand how a human being is like a storm.

Like metaphors, similes work by comparison, but with the word *like* or *as*, similes indicate their comparisons more explicitly. Similes announce the relationship between the tenor and vehicle more formally. When, after the shipwreck, Alonso rejects Gonzalo's attempts to comfort him, Sebastian speaks a simile when he comments about Alonso that,

He receives comfort like cold porridge. (2.1.10-11)

Here Sebastian is talking about the way Alonso responds to Gonzalo's efforts to cheer him up after the shipwreck and transports *cold porridge* to describe Alonso's reaction to Gonzalo's *comfort*. You could chart the simile:

vehicle	:	tenor
cold porridge	:	comfort

The metaphor that opens Sonnet 68 articulates both tenor and vehicle—the cheek and the map—and makes clear their relationship: the cheek "is" the map. Sometimes, however, a metaphor does not name both tenor and vehicle. Or sometimes a metaphor does not state so clearly how the vehicle corresponds to the tenor. Such metaphors require more interpretation. Consider, for example, Ferdinand's promise:

> The white cold virgin snow upon my heart
> Abates the ardor of my liver. (4.1.55-6)

We know that Ferdinand speaks a metaphor because *snow* cannot have fallen literally upon his *heart*. But Ferdinand doesn't say explicitly what is affecting his heart that corresponds to "virgin snow," so we need to interpret.

First, some definitions:

- *Virgin*, when used as an adjective, can mean "comparable to a virgin in respect of purity or freedom from stain; pure, unstained, unsullied" (*OED* 14a). Thus, we might understand "virgin snow" to mean snow just fallen, not yet dirty or melting.

- In Shakespeare's day the *liver* was "the bodily organ regarded as the seat of love or other passionate emotion, as anger, bitterness, etc." (*OED* 4a). The *heart* was considered "the seat of emotions generally" (*OED* 9a) and "the seat of love and affection" (*OED* 10a).

- *Ardor* means "fierce or burning heat" (*OED* 1) and also the "heat of passion or desire" (*OED* 3).

We can start interpreting the metaphor by charting:

vehicle	:	tenor
virgin snow	:	?

Then, we can make a logical interpretation based on the context of Ferdinand's statement. Sometimes that context suggests more than one interpretation. For instance, we could say:

vehicle	:	tenor
virgin snow	:	first love

Or we could say:

vehicle	:	tenor
virgin snow	:	love free of sexual desire

Sometimes a statement or speech articulates more than one part of a metaphor's vehicle or tenor. Take, for example, Antonio's comment as he tries to persuade Sebastian to kill King Alonso and to seize the crown. It includes several vehicles associated with tides:

> *Antonio*   Ebbing men, indeed
> (Most often) do so near the bottom run
> By their own fear or sloth. (2.1.220-2)

Here are four steps that can help lead to an accurate and productive analysis of such a metaphor. I have included sample analysis for each step.

STEP 1. IDENTIFY THE METAPHOR'S SPEAKER, AUDIENCE, & CONTEXT.

Jot down speaker and audience, and briefly review the immediate and relevant context of the speech.

Example:

> Antonio to Sebastian. King Alonso has fallen asleep, and Antonio tells Sebastian that his "imagination sees a crown / Dropping upon [Sebastian's] head" (2.1.202-3).

STEP 2. IDENTIFY THE METAPHOR'S VEHICLES.

Underline all the elements of the metaphor's vehicle in the speech.

> *You can find a metaphor's vehicle by looking for the parts that would be absurd if taken literally with the tenor. Here you can recognize that "ebbing" is part of the vehicle because it would be absurd to imagine that Antonio is talking literally about men in the ocean affected by the tide.*

Example:

> *Antonio*   <u>Ebbing</u> men, indeed
> (Most often) do so <u>near the bottom run</u>
> By their own fear or sloth.

STEP 3. SORT THE METAPHOR'S VEHICLE & TENOR.

A. Start by listing the elements of the vehicle and tenor the speaker states explicitly. Leave blank spaces for the corresponding parts of the vehicle and tenor implied.

Example:

vehicle	:	tenor
ebbing	:	? _____
? _____	:	men
near the bottom	:	? _____
run	:	? _____

B. Then, think about the analogies and fill in those blanks.

You might find it helpful to identify the worlds of the vehicle and the tenor. For instance, the vehicle here is from the world of oceans and the tenor is from the world of society.

As you think about the analogies, be sure to review the full list of meanings of any key words. Although ebb means "to flow back or recede, as the water of a tidal sea or river" (OED 1), ebb also can be said, "Of a ship: To sink with the tide" (OED 1b). This second meaning of ebb helps us make sense of the metaphor's vehicle as describing a ship sailing nearer the bottom of the ocean when the tide is low.

As you identify missing parts of the vehicle, you might find it helpful to ask yourself questions like, "What literally would be ebbing and run near the bottom?"

As you try to understand the tenor, you might find it helpful to ask yourself questions like: "What quality of men would be like ships ebbing with the tide?" Or: "In what condition would a man be that is like a ship's running near the bottom of the ocean?"

Use all of the clues the text provides. In this passage "By their own fear or sloth" leads us to understand that "ebbing" men could be interpreted as unambitious.

Remember that filling in the blanks requires interpretation and that there may be more than one way to interpret accurately.

Example:

vehicle (world of oceans & tides)	:	tenor (world of society & status)
ebbing	:	unambitious
ships	:	men
near the bottom (of the ocean)	:	near the bottom of society
run	:	live

STEP 4. ARTICULATE THE METAPHOR'S MEANINGS & IMPLICATIONS.

First, think carefully about the metaphor's specific vehicle. In the case of this metaphor, think about the qualities of tides—of ebbing and flowing. Then, think about how the qualities of the vehicle are transported onto the metaphor's tenor.

Keep in mind that not all of the implications and meanings of a metaphor are necessarily intended by the character who speaks the metaphor. Even if a metaphor's implications are not intended by a character, they nonetheless can acquire meaning in the play.

Example:

> Antonio's metaphor compares an unambitious Sebastian to an ebbing ship that floats closer to the bottom of the ocean because the tide has ebbed—or gone out. Antonio's metaphor suggests that being an unambitious man will naturally leave Sebastian nearer the bottom of society just as an ebb tide will naturally leave a ship in shallower water and, thus, closer to the ocean's bottom. Antonio is attempting to convince Sebastian to seize the crown by killing his brother, the current King Alonso, thereby raising himself to the highest position in society. However, Antonio's metaphor also implies that men cannot control their position in society. If ships literally will be raised and lowered from the ocean's bottom by the tides that naturally ebb and flow, then the metaphor suggests that men figuratively will be raised and lowered from society's bottom by some social or political "tide." Antonio's metaphor unwittingly suggests that cyclical forces beyond men's control cause men to become more and less powerful.

85

Whereas metaphor and simile work by comparison, metonymy and synecdoche work by association or scale.

> One thing standing for another associated thing is called **METONYMY**.

Stephano uses metonymy when he tells Trinculo, "keep a good tongue in thy head" (3.2.108). A *tongue* is associated with speech, and "a good tongue" stands here for speaking appropriately or well.

> Part of a thing standing for the whole thing is called **SYNECDOCHE**.

Prospero uses synecdoche when he warns Ferdinand that if he has sex with Miranda before the marriage ceremony, then "barren hate, / Sour-eyed disdain, and discord, shall bestrew / The union of your bed with weeds so loathly" (4.1.19-21). The *union of your bed* is part of the *marriage*, and, thus, Prospero warns Ferdinand that premarital sex will result in a hateful and childless marriage.

The difference between *being associated with* and *being part of* can be very slim, so it can be difficult to decide whether to classify a figure of speech as metonymy or synecdoche. The difference between metonymy and metaphor, however, is larger and more significant. In order to understand a metaphor or simile we need to imagine how a tenor in one world compares to a vehicle from a distant world: we need to imagine how one thing *is* or *is like* another thing with which it ordinarily is not associated. Unlike metaphor and simile, metonymy and synecdoche are from the same world as the things they stand for.

APPENDIX 3. ON HOW AN EDITION OF *THE TEMPEST* IS MADE

Shakespeare, who died in 1616, did not take part in the publication of his plays. The earliest extant text of *The Tempest* is found in a collection of Shakespeare's plays entitled *Mr. William Shakespeares Comedies, Histories, & Tragedies*, which was printed in London in 1623. Scholars now refer to this first edition of Shakespeare's collected plays as the *First Folio*, and all editions of *The Tempest* are based on it. You can compare your edition of *The Tempest* to the text included in the First Folio by finding a facsimile of it in your library or on the World Wide Web.

You will notice a number of differences between the First Folio and any modern edition of the play.

- **Editors standardize spelling and punctuation according to current practices.** So, for instance, the First Folio's lines,

> *Mira.* If by your Art (my deerest father) you haue
> Put the wild waters in this Rore;alay them:

become in most modern editions,

> *Miranda*   If by your art, my dearest father, you have
>   Put the wild waters in this roar, allay them.

- **Editors add stage directions not in the First Folio.** Often editors distinguish their own stage directions from those in the First Folio by enclosing them in parentheses or brackets. For instance, in act 5, scene 1, the Boatswain reports that their ship, which had been wrecked, has been found in as good condition as when they first had sailed. When, upon hearing the report on the magically restored ship, Ariel says, "Sir, all this service / Have I done since I went," the First Folio does not include a stage direction. Many modern editors, however, include "(*aside to Prospero*)" or "[*to Prospero*]" before Ariel's line. Editors base such stage directions on their reading of the play, so you should always test them by reading the lines closely and considering other possible stagings.

- **Editors add line numbers.** Although the First Folio divides the play into acts and scenes, it does not mark line numbers. Because some speeches in the play are in prose, not verse, a modern edition's line numbers vary depending on the size of the page. (*See "Listening for Meter" for explanations of verse and prose.*)

- **Editors include notes that explain selected words and phrases.** In some notes editors provide definitions for words whose meanings were different in Shakespeare's day or whose meanings might be unfamiliar to us now. For instance, editors often note that the word *yarely* means "quickly" or "promptly" and that the word *luggage* means "what has to be lugged about"—not necessarily only by travellers. Editors do not list all possible definitions, but you can check the *Oxford English Dictionary* for a complete list of seventeenth-century meanings of any word. In other notes editors may offer more extensive explanations of the meaning of a phrase or a line. Read such notes critically: there may be additional ways to understand the phrase or line.

ACKNOWLEDGMENTS

Over the years I have had the pleasure of reading Shakespeare's plays with hundreds of students at Friends Seminary. Their enthusiastic interest in the plays, their willingness to work to understand them, and their fresh interpretations have inspired me to develop and publish this series of guides. It has been a special pleasure to work with Friends Seminary alumna Lauren Simkin Berke who has designed the book's cover with inimitable vision, wit, and craft. I am once again grateful to Robert Lauder, Principal of Friends Seminary, for his gracious support of this project and to my English Department colleagues for their enduring camaraderie and help.

I am grateful to Donna Anstey at Yale University Press for granting me permission to include, on page 87 of this guide, the scanned image of two lines of *The Tempest* from the 1954 Yale University Press facsimile edition of *Mr. William Shakespeares Comedies, Histories, & Tragedies*.

Special thanks goes to Heather Cross, who convinced me to make the guides available to the general public, who made key suggestions about their structure, and who responded generously to many questions. I am indebted to Jim Windolf for the question about social hierarchy that concludes each scene's questions: it is adapted from one he wrote for a Steinbeck novel we taught together some years ago. I am grateful to Chris Doire, Josh Goren, Philip Kay, Cara Murray, Thomas O'Connell, Katherine Olson, and Craig Saslow for their valuable comments on the guides' preface and appendices and to Sarah Spieldenner for her excellent suggestions about the entire guide. My ongoing exchanges with Patrick Morrissey about meter and figurative language were vital to the development of the appendices, and his careful reading of the entire manuscript greatly improved the guide's clarity and accuracy. Finally, I am grateful to Gordon Minette for his advice on matters large and small as I prepared *A Guide to Reading Shakespeare's The Tempest* for publication.

Made in the USA
Lexington, KY
26 October 2013